Every Day
and Sunday, Too

Text by Gail Ramshaw

Art by Judy Jarrett

Augsburg

Minneapolis

Glossary of liturgical actions appears at the end of the book.

EVERY DAY AND SUNDAY, TOO

Scripture quotations, unless otherwise noted, are from the New Revised Standard Version Bible © 1989 Division of Christian Education of the National Council of the Churches of Christ in the U.S.A. Used by permission.

Cover design: David Meyer
Interior design: Circus Design

Library of Congress Cataloging-in-Publication Data
Ramshaw, Gail, 1947–
    Every day and Sunday, too / written by Gail Ramshaw ; illustrated
by Judy Jarrett.
        p.   cm.
    Summary: Links church liturgy to everyday activities, using
illustrations with brief text and scriptural passages.
    ISBN 0-8066-2334-9 (alk. paper)
    1. Children--Religious life. 2. Worship--Juvenile literature.
[1. Christian life. 2. Worship.] I. Jarrett, Judy, ill.
II. Title.
BV4571.R35   1996
264'.041'083--DC20   96-21178
                                                                  CIP
                                                                   AC

The paper used in this publication meets the minimum requirements of American National Standard for Information Sciences—Permanence of Paper for Printed Library Materials, ANSI Z329.48-1984. ∞ ™

Printed in Hong Kong   ISBN 0-8066-2334-9   10-23349

01 00 99 98 97 2 3 4 5 6 7 8

Introduction

At first glance, the words and images of this book seem to speak of daily life: gathering for a meal, sitting on a hillside, going on a picnic, listening to a bedtime story, or celebrating a birthday party. In Judy Jarrett's delightful art and Gail Ramshaw's engaging words, everyday actions appear to be the central focus of this book.

But take another look, and you will see that the order of the book reveals the fundamental structure of Christian worship. Christians gather on Sunday, sing with one voice, ask forgiveness, read from the Bible, listen to a preacher, pray for the needs of the world, bring gifts to the table, offer a great prayer of thanksgiving, eat and drink, receive God's blessing, and depart in peace. This common pattern is shared by many Christians throughout the world. It is the pattern of gathering with Christ, hearing him speak through scripture, receiving his bread and cup, and going forth to announce his presence, a pattern alluded to in Luke 24:13-35.

Here the actions of daily life and the Sunday assembly are placed side-by-side as a way to see every day in light of Sunday and to see again Sunday's gathering as a way of life for every day. For instance, on the page entitled "Giving thanks at table" you see a family saying a table prayer before eating the meal. They are offering thanks to God for the gifts of food and life. But what else might they be saying? And what do you say at your table? On this page, as on every page, there is a scripture citation. Here, Psalm 92:1 appears on the refrigerator. Look up the text in the Bible, and you will find words that interpret the action and invite you to do the same: give thanks to the Lord! But do you notice what that fluffy dog sees in the distance? Beyond the window, the assembly is gathered at the altar-table to give thanks for the gifts of bread and wine, the body and blood of Christ. What do the two thanksgivings have to do with each other? Perhaps the words and artwork are inviting the reader to see an everyday meal as an extension of sharing in Christ's bread and cup.

One of the basic questions we can never stop asking is this: What does it mean to be a Christian today? It is an important question for our children. One ancient answer to the contemporary question is found in the liturgy. Christians gather to learn again and again the actions of Christ, so that we might be Christ every day and Sunday, too. Here are words and images that help us learn who we have become in baptism. Read these fine words and look for surprising details in the artwork. Help your children speak about the ordinary, joyful, and sad experiences of daily life and Christ's presence with them. You may even want to bring this book with you to the Sunday assembly as a friendly guide.

Be welcome, then, to the many treasures on these pages.

Snails live in shells one by one, but we people are creatures who like being together. We want to see our friends often, every day, or at least once a week.

ISAIAH 61:10

Like a dogwood tree that changes its color each season of the year, people dress in different outfits depending on the day and the weather. It's good that we don't have to look the same summer and winter, happy or sad.

Lighting candles

We light candles at special meals, on birthday cakes, on window sills in wintertime. Candles shine up the room like stars sparkle up the sky.

Tthere's lots going on in our lives, sometimes too much. It's good to sit quietly for awhile. Like a mother bird waiting for her eggs to hatch, we get ready for new things to happen.

Confessing sin

When we've done something wrong,
we admit it, we say we're sorry, and try to do
better next time. It's that simple. It's that hard.
Maybe when cats lick each other after a fight,
they are saying they're sorry.

Birds and dolphins sing messages to one another. We people have fun singing together. We sing favorite songs that mean something important, over and over again. But we sing new ones, too.

PSALM 149:1

Listening to scripture

When the family gets together, grandparents may tell about life in the old days. When night comes, we listen to our favorite bedtime stories. All these stories help us understand who we are, how things are different, how things are the same.

Life isn't easy. We need other people to hug us when we cry, to be with us when we're afraid, to help us do what we have to do, to get us down from the tree if we climbed up too high.

Everything needs water to live. We water our plants, we leave out water for the pets, we walk through puddles. We floated in water before we were born. We wash ourselves and each other every day.

Welcoming

Remember what it's like to arrive at the home of an old friend or a relative? The door opens and just as your friend or grandparent sees you, a big smile appears. Welcome! Come on in!

PSALM 145:15-16

Praying for others

Every day we receive things from others—a drink of water, our allowance, help from a doctor. A cow moos to be milked, we ask for extra blankets and somehow, even the soil asks God for rain.

Greeting each other in peace

People have many ways to greet each other: a wave, a pat on the back, a kiss, a handshake, jumping up and down together. We get closer to one another, to show that our hearts are trying to touch.

Like sharing food with friends at a picnic, we give some of what is ours to others. Sometimes, like a mama cat nursing her newborn kittens, we give more than things or money: we give ourselves for the good of others.

When we expect visitors for a meal, we clean up our homes and set the table with a cloth. Sometimes we add flowers and candles so that when we're ready to eat, the table welcomes us brightly.

Standing up

When something very important happens, we want to know what's going on. Our heads want to be up high, and our legs want to jump. We are too excited to stay sitting. There are times when we even wish we could fly up into the air to get the best view.

Giving thanks

One of the differences between people and squirrels is that people say thanks when they receive something. We say thanks for candy, thanks for letting me play in your yard, thanks for the homework help, thanks for the weird present! Thanks, thanks, thanks.

We know about some things we can't see,
like the sun behind the clouds, the pouring rain at night,
the secret of a friend, the love of our families.
Many important things in life are beyond our sight.

PSALM 148:1-2

Eating and drinking

All living things must eat—the elephants, the wolves, the frogs, the cockroaches. Eating keeps us all alive. But sharing a simple meal keeps us really alive and makes us open-hearted.

At the end of the day, at the end of our lives, when school is over, we say goodbye. With a wave or a hug or a touch, we signal that we'll be back and that we want each other safe until then.

The pattern of Sunday worship: a glossary of liturgical actions

Meeting on Sunday   Christians gather on Sunday, the day of resurrection, when the crucified and risen Christ appeared to his disciples. Toward the end of their gospels, Matthew, Luke, and John relate numerous appearances of the risen Christ.

Dressing ourselves   When Christians are baptized, they are clothed in a white robe. The white robe, or alb, is also worn by persons who lead worship, a sign for the community of its baptism into Christ. Ordained presiders may wear a stole and chasuble ("little house") at the celebration of the eucharist. The colors reflect the changing feasts and seasons of the year.

Lighting candles   In worship, Christians prefer to use real candles with "living" flames. Ordinary white candles mark a liturgical center such as the altar. A baptismal candle is a sign of the light of Christ. The tall paschal candle is first used at the Easter Vigil and then burns by the baptismal font or pool during the rest of the year. It is an image of Christ's resurrection and the flame of the Holy Spirit.

Keeping silence   Maintaining an intentional silence in the liturgy and in daily life allows people to hear with greater attentiveness. It is one important way in which Christians listen for the voice of Christ speaking to them.

Confessing sin   Christians are able to confess their sins—to speak the truth about their failings—because they know that God is ready to forgive and heal them. In this action, Christ invites his followers to be forgiving people in daily life.

Singing   Singing together creates one voice and draws people into a common action. Singing gives praise to God, expresses faith, and carries the Christian vision. Everyone should be free to sing, whether young or old, well-trained or an amateur.

Listening to scripture   The first major part of the liturgy centers on the proclamation of scripture and our response to it. Through these ancient stories,

God continues to speak to us today. They proclaim God's care for the people of Israel (the Hebrew Bible), God's activity among the first Christians (the New Testament letters), and God's presence in Jesus (the four Gospel books).

Hearing the sermon   The person who preaches speaks the good news in light of the biblical readings and contemporary life. The preacher helps us understand that God is always with us every day: caring for us, helping us, and calling us back to God's love.

Baptizing   Many churches celebrate baptism after the sermon, the preacher leading the people from scripture to the font. Here the church celebrates new birth in Christ and welcomes brothers and sisters into the household of faith. Some churches baptize by pouring water over the head, while others immerse the person in a baptismal pool.

Welcoming   After the washing, the newly-baptized may be marked with the sign of the cross in oil on the forehead, clothed in a white robe, and given a candle. They are anointed or marked with oil as a sign of their union with Jesus, the Anointed One. The worshiping assembly then welcomes its new brothers and sisters.

Praying for others   The reading of scripture and the preaching lead us to pray for the needs of the church, the world, the sick, and the poor. With confident faith, the church asks for God's mercy on all who are in need or suffer in any way.

Greeting each other in peace   In these words, we hear the voice of the risen Christ and we offer that same greeting of peace to each other. It is also our commitment to be a people of peace, forgiveness, and healing. In some churches, this greeting takes place before the communion.

Giving   Ancient Christians would bring more than enough bread and wine for the eucharist, the rest being given to the poor and needy. Today we present the gifts of bread and wine, as well as our gifts of money that will help the needy and the church's life. We offer what God has first given us, our selves, our time, and our possessions.

Setting the table   As the community prepares to celebrate the Lord's Supper, the table is made ready. After the gifts of bread and wine have been presented, a brief prayer is said, announcing our purpose in gathering at the table.

Standing up   In worship, Christ speaks to the church in countless ways. But there are two central proclamations at which we always stand: the gospel reading at the pulpit, or ambo, and the great thanksgiving at the table. Our standing signals the importance of these moments.

Giving thanks at table   The church follows the actions of Jesus, who, at his last supper, blessed God for the gifts of bread and wine. The presider speaks or sings for us all and praises God for the gift of creation, God's faithfulness to Israel, and the life, death, and resurrection of Christ. We ask God to send the Spirit upon the gifts and those who share them. We conclude the thanksgiving with the Hebrew word "amen" and then pray the Lord's Prayer.

Praising with angels   During the thanksgiving at table, we sing the great song of God's glory, the Sanctus. It is the union of two songs, one from the Hebrew Bible (Isaiah 6:3) and one from the New Testament (Matthew 21:9). It is a song of praise and an announcement of Christ's coming to us in the eucharist.

Eating and drinking   After the Lord's Prayer, we come to the table and share the bread and cup. We come to the feast that proclaims Christ's triumph over death and his care for our hungry world. We are fed by Christ, joined to each other, and strengthened to be his servants in daily life.

Going forth   In this pattern of worship we discover what it means to be a Christian in the world. We gather with the community of faith, hear the good news, pray for ourselves and the needy, and receive God's love in Christ's supper. We now go forth with God's blessing to speak with hope, to care for the needy, to be people of peace, and to share our love with one another.